ELSTON ©

For HIGHWOOD,
All THE BEST.

Dave

ELSTON'S HAT TRICK

POLESTAR

BOOK PUBLISHERS

Elston's Hat Trick
for Sybil

Published by
Polestar Press Ltd.
RR # 1 Winlaw, BC, V0G 2J0
and
2758 Charles Street
Vancouver, BC, V5K 3A7

Cover design by Jim Brennan
Author photo by Rob Evans
Produced by Michelle Benjamin, Jim Brennan, and Julian Ross
Printed in Canada by Best-Gagne Book Manufacturers

Acknowledgements
Thanks to Bill Davidson.
These cartoons have previously appeared in *The Calgary Sun*, *Inside Hockey*, *The Hockey News*, and *The Edmonton Sun*.

Original Cartoons
If you are interested in purchasing an original Elston, or in corresponding with Dave Elston, you can write to him c/o Calgary Sun, 2615-12th St. N.E., Calgary, Alberta T2E 7W9

Canadian Cataloguing in Publication Data

Elston, Dave, 1958-
Elston's hat trick
ISBN 0-919591-86-8
1. Hockey--Caricatures and Cartoons. 2. Sports--Caricatures and cartoons. 3. Canadian wit and humor, Pictorial. 1. Title
NC1449.E48A4 1993   741.5'971   C93-091688-3

CONTENTS

1991-92 REGULAR SEASON HIGHLIGHTS

ST. LOUIS GENERAL MANAGER RON CARON LOSES DEFENSEMAN SCOTT STEVENS AS COMPENSATION FOR SIGNING FREE AGENT BRENDAN SHANAHAN.

RON CARON

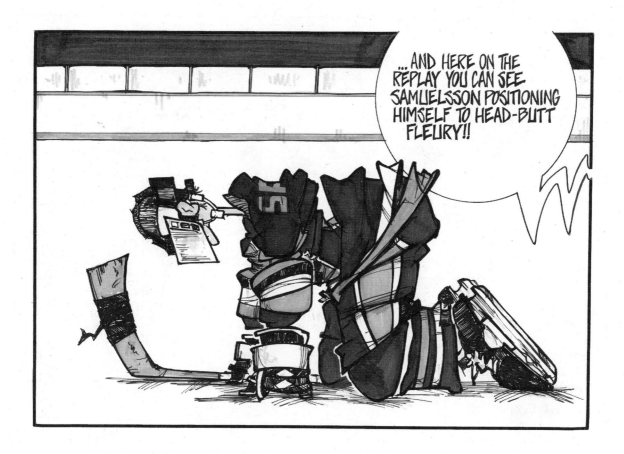

JANUARY 2, 1992:
DOUG RISEBROUGH TRADES DOUG GILMOUR TO TORONTO.

BILL RANFORD

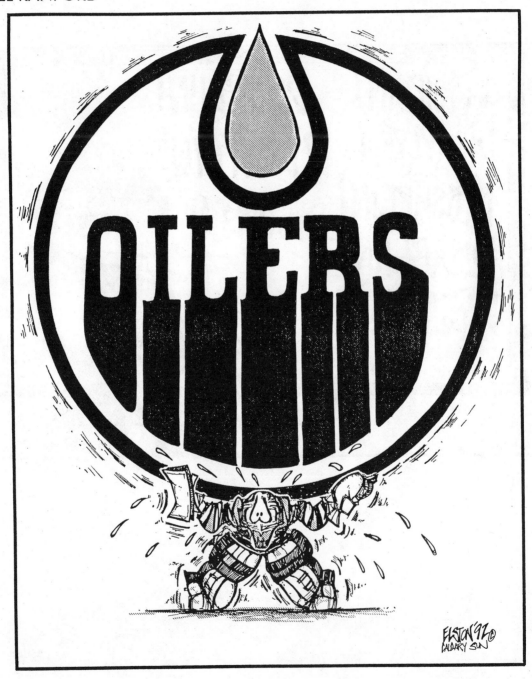

MARCH 26, 1992:
AL MACINNIS' SLAPSHOT SHATTERS THE GLASS AT THE SADDLEDOME.

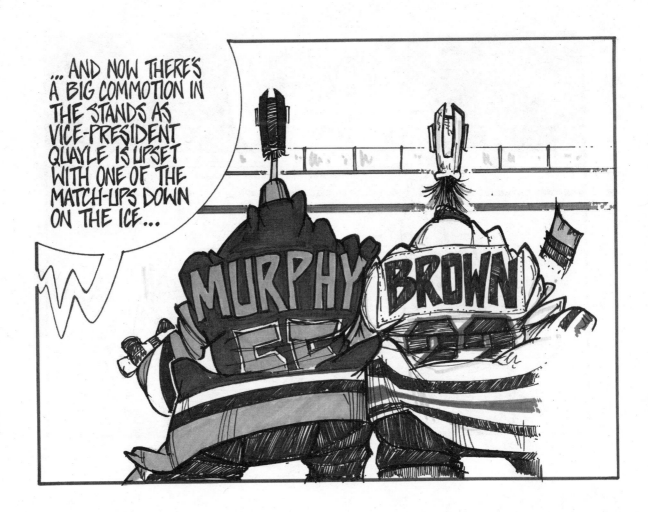

THE 20-48-12 NORDIQUES

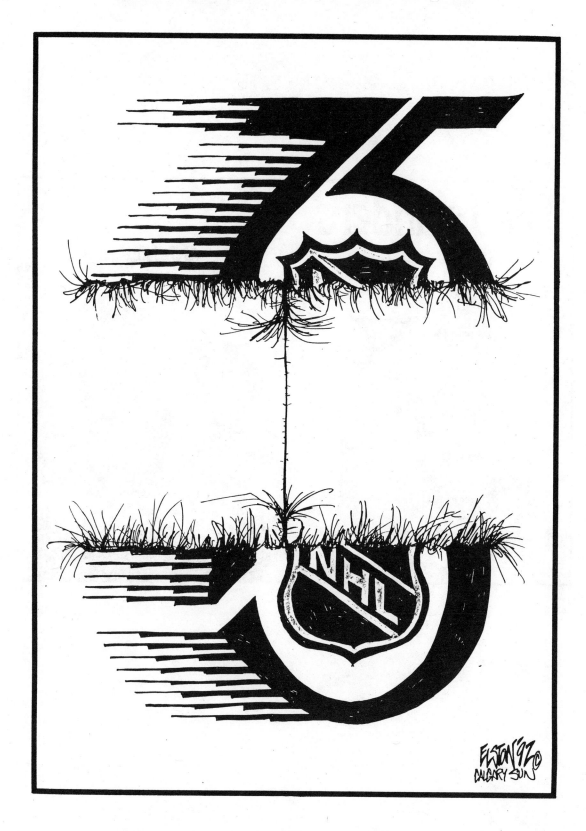

THE FUNNY ONE
VS
THE NEXT ONE

FEBRUARY 18, 1992:
ERIC LINDROS SCORES IN SHOOTOUT TO BEAT GERMANY 4-3.

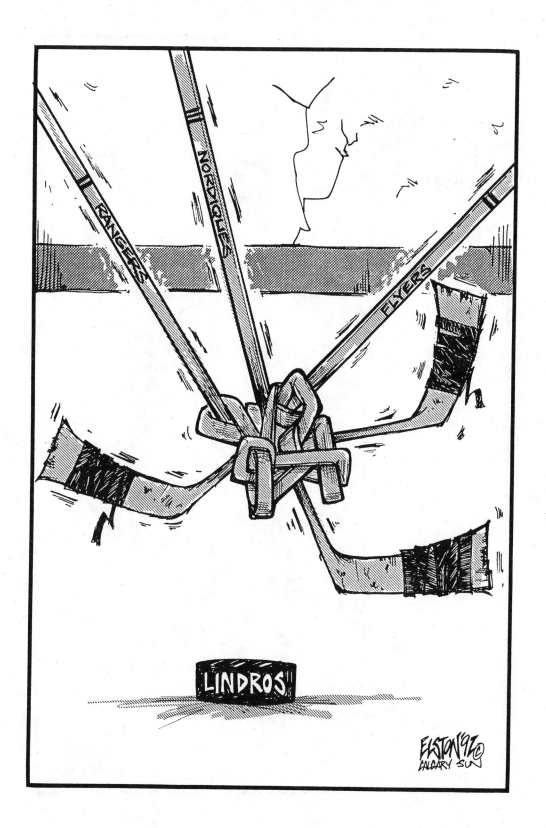

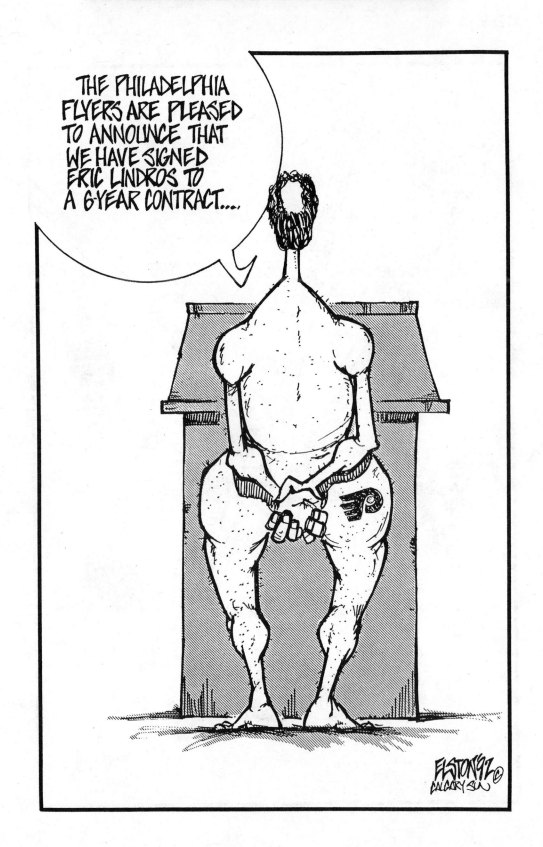

WIDE WORLD
OF ELSTON

SEPTEMBER 13, 1991:
A CHUNK OF CONCRETE THE SIZE OF A LOCOMOTIVE FALLS OFF OF
OLYMPIC STADIUM.

B.C. LIONS OWNER MURRAY PEZIM PRESENTS CALGARY STAMPEDERS
OWNER LARRY RYCKMAN WITH A PACIFIER AT HALFTIME:
B.C. 31 / CALGARY 15.
FINAL SCORE:
CALGARY 43 / B.C. 41.

SUPER BOWL XXV1:
BUFFALO'S THURMAN THOMAS MISSES THE START OF THE GAME
AFTER MISPLACING HIS HELMET.

NOVEMBER 15, 1992—COMMONWEALTH STADIUM:
WESTERN DIVISION SEMI-FINAL—SASKATCHEWAN'S DAVE RIDGWAY
SLIPS AND MISSES A LAST-MINUTE FIELD GOAL.
FINAL SCORE:
EDMONTON 22
SASKATCHEWAN 20

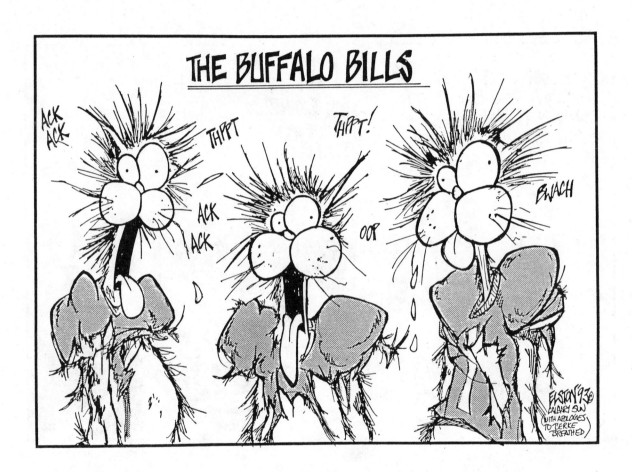

NEWS ITEM:
MUCH TO THE CHAGRIN OF SOME TOP COMPETITORS, CANADA
DECIDES TO HOLD SELECTION EVENTS PRIOR TO THE ALBERTVILLE
OLYMPICS.

GROUP PICTURE OF THE CANADIAN
MEN'S DOWNHILL TEAM

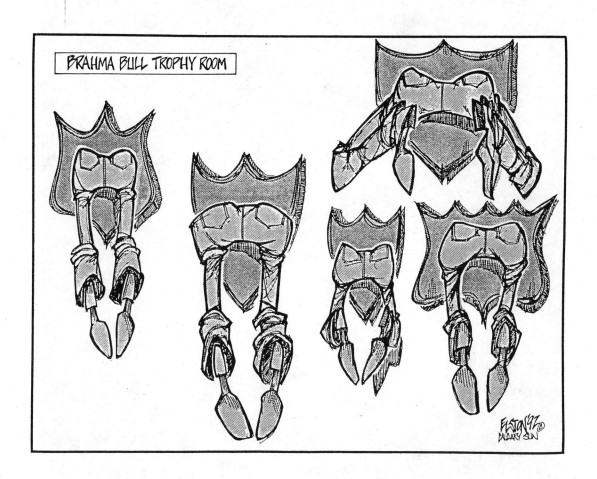

BRAHMA BULL TROPHY ROOM

THE MARK OF EXCELLENCE

1992-93
REGULAR SEASON
HIGHLIGHTS

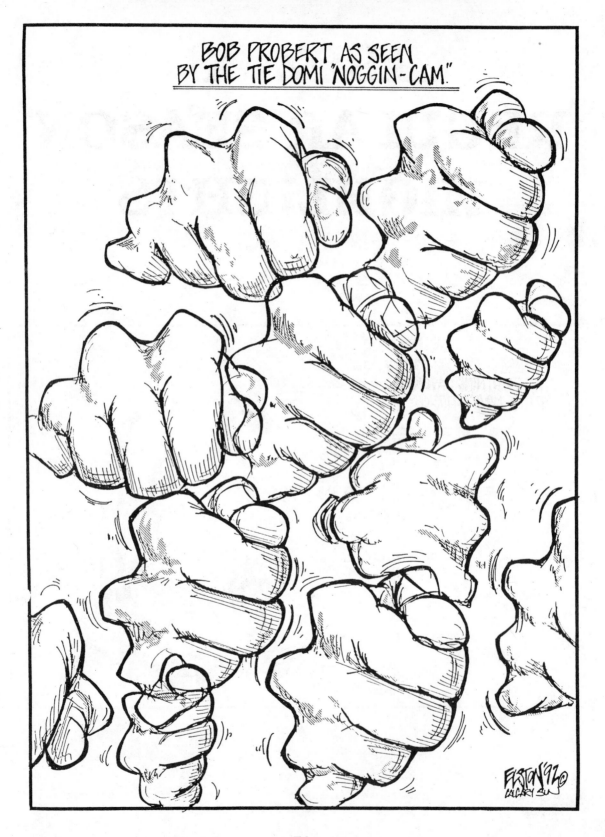

TIM HUNTER SELECTED BY TAMPA BAY
IN EXPANSION DRAFT

MANON RHEAUME LANDS TRYOUT WITH TAMPA BAY LIGHTNING.

JANUARY 12, 1993:
MARIO LEMIEUX IS DIAGNOSED WITH HODGKINS DISEASE.

BRENT ASHTON PLAYING FOR HIS NINTH NHL TEAM.

MINOR HOCKEY WEEK.

BEST OF THE 1993 PLAYOFF SERIES

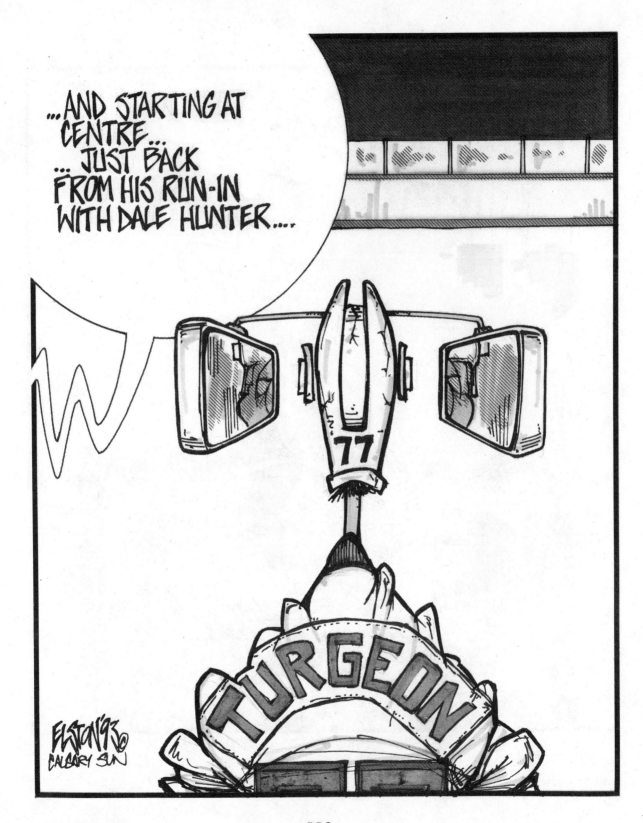

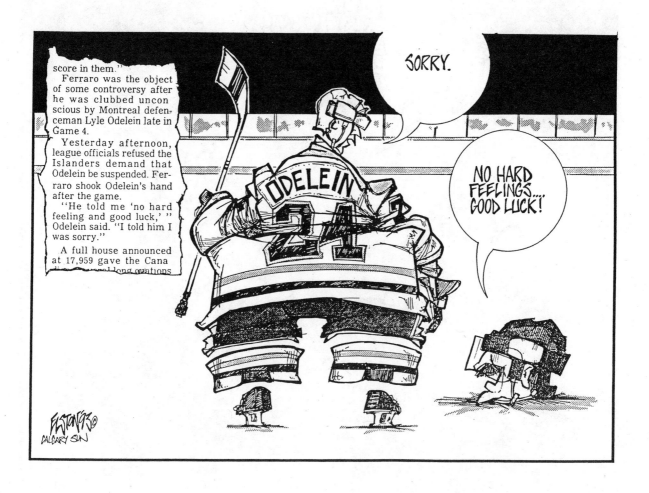